Materials and Techniques

Felt and Paper

Alot of the projects use felt and construction paper. Most craft shops carry the 9″ x 12″ pieces of felt in a variety of colors. Construction paper can be found where school and stationery supplies are sold.

Paint

Acrylic craft paint is the best paint to use for these projects. Your local craft shop can help you to find this type of paint. This paint is permanent when dry and is easy for the children to use. The colors are premixed and can be used directly from the jar. Any spills should be cleaned up before the paint dries. This type of paint does not have to be sealed afterward. If you use a paint such as tempera, the piece will need to be sealed with a wood sealer or acrylic finish after the paint has dried because the paint is not permanent and will come off or run when touched with water. Sealing will keep this from happening.

She's An Angel Plaque

Pictured on Page 4

Materials

28, 5″ wooden forks
White craft glue
Lightweight cardboard
Pink index card
Acrylic paints: blue, white, pink, yellow
Markers or crayons: red, black
Picture hanger

Instructions

1. See Fig. 1 for sizes of fork parts. You will need to cut 6 A-parts, 13 C-parts, 4 E-parts, 3 F-parts, 2 H-parts, and one J-part. Save all the handle ends (parts B, D, and G) to use for the other parts. The forks can be cut with scissors, but this should to be done by an adult for younger children.
2. For the lower skirt, arrange 6 A-parts as shown in Fig. 2 and glue 5 B-parts on top of them. Gluing the B-parts atop the A-parts will hold all the pieces together.
3. For the middle skirt, arrange 5 C-parts as shown in Fig. 3 and glue 4 G-parts on top of them.
4. For the top skirt, arrange 4 E-parts as shown in Fig. 4 and glue 3 F-parts on top of them.
5. For the bodice, glue the edges of 3 D-parts together as shown in Fig. 5. Glue 2 more D-parts in place for the upper arms. Cut 2 more G-parts and glue in place for the lower arms.

Continued on Page 5

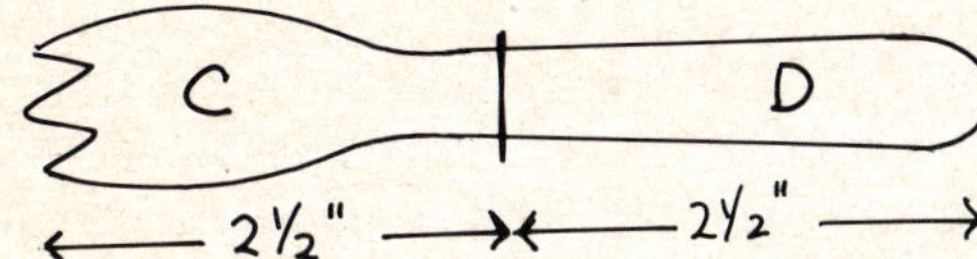
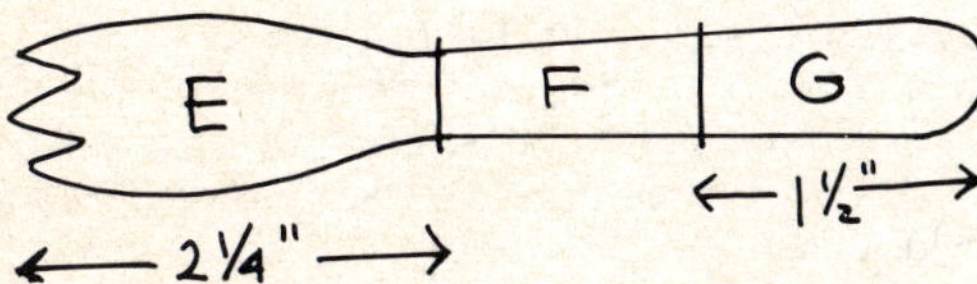
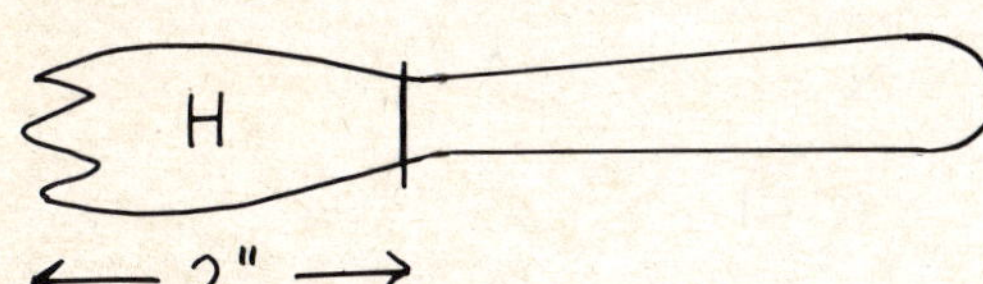
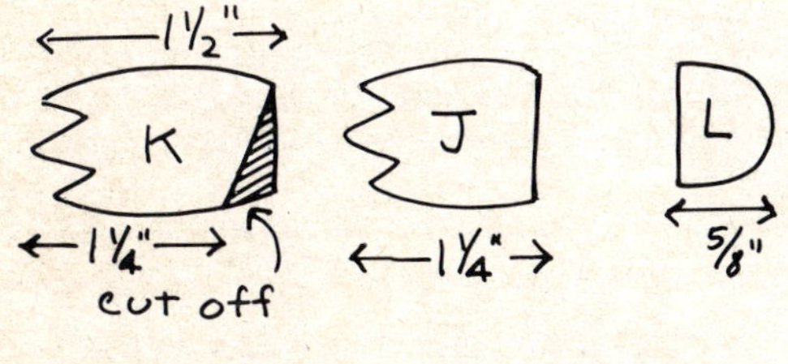
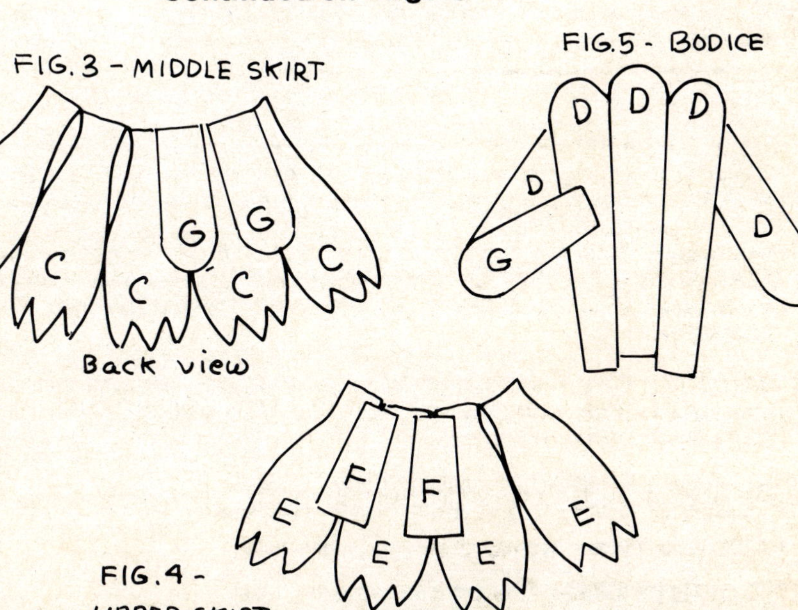

THE CHRISTIAN WAY OF LIFE
268 I Am His a
George Wade Robinson, 1838-1877
1. Loved with ev - er - last - ing
2. Heav'n a - bove is
3. Things that once were
4. His for - ev

Spir - it, brea
Some-thing i
Closed in ev - er
Ah, with what

Oh, this full and per - fect peace! Oh, this trans - port
Birds with glad - der songs o'er - flow, Flow'rs with deep - er
Oh, to lie for - ev - er here, Doubt, and care, a
Heav'n and earth may fade and flee, First-born light

In
Since
While
But wh

He Is Mine
James

Are Blott   Know!

PRAISE AND TESTIMONY
269
Merrill Dunlop, b. 1905

are blot - ted
tha   blot - ted
ll blot - ted

know!
know! My sins
know!"

My
oy, My
sing "My

'now!
I know!

know! I
the

She's An Angel Plaque

6. For one wing, glue the edges of three D-parts together as shown in Fig. 6. Glue 4 C-parts to the back of it as shown. Turn this wing over and use it as a guide for making the second wing in the same way.
7. From lightweight cardboard, cut one head and one neck, using the patterns. For the hair, glue 2 H-parts and one J-part to the head as shown in Fig. 7.
8. For the top of the hair, cut 2 fork ends 1½″ long and then cut them at an angle as shown in Fig. 1; this makes the K-parts. Glue 2 K-parts in place as shown in Fig. 8.
9. Following Fig. 9, glue the head to the neck. Glue the neck to the back of the bodice. Also glue the wings to the back of the bodice. Glue the lower skirt to the back of the middle skirt so that middle skirt overlaps top of lower skirt, and glue the upper skirt to the front of the middle skirt so that upper skirt overlaps top of middle skirt.
10. For the hands, cut handle ends ⅝″ long— see L-parts in Fig. 1. A craft knife may be required to cut such a short piece without splitting the fork; an adult should do this. Glue the hands to the ends of the arms so they touch each other at the center. The hands should not be glued flat against the bodice; glue the back edges to the angel so hands angle outward.
11. Paint the face pink, the hair yellow, the wings white, and the dress blue. Use markers or crayons to draw the face, following the face on the head pattern. To make white dots for trim on the dress, dip the handle of a paint brush into white paint and touch it to the dress where each dot goes.
12. Cut the book from a pink index card using the book pattern. Fold it on the broken line and glue it behind the angel's hands.
13. Attach a picture hanger to the back.

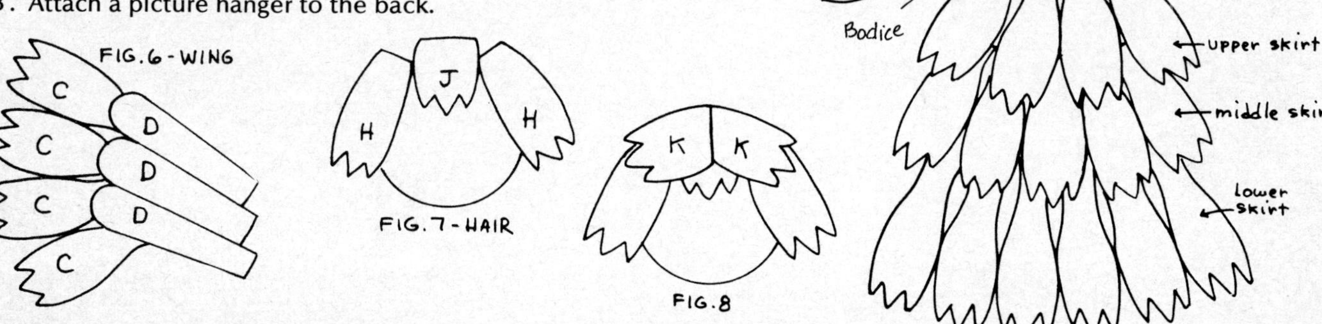

Hideaway Pets

Materials (Per Pet)

Wooden napkin ring, 1¾″ dia. x 1¼″ wide
Lg. (36.5 mm) wooden head bead
Lightweight cardboard
Craft glue
Acrylic paints: brown, tan, and black plus rose paint for bear and white paint for puppy

Instructions

1. For the body, glue a napkin ring to a small piece of lightweight cardboard as shown in Fig. 1. When the glue is dry, trim the cardboard to fit.
2. Cut 2 ears from lightweight cardboard, using the pattern, and glue them to the head bead. If you wish to use the heads as lids or little containers, do not glue the head beads in place; simply sit them in place. Otherwise, you may glue them on if desired.
3. Painting the bear: Paint the bear brown with tan ears. Make black dots or eyes and his nose by dipping the handle of a paint brush in black paint and touching it to his face. Paint a tiny rose mouth and rose heart on his chest. Add rose dots for trim on body and ears. Add white highlight dots on his eyes.
4. Painting the puppy: Paint the puppy tan with brown spots. Make his ace the same as for the bear (step 3) and add trim of white dots on his spots.

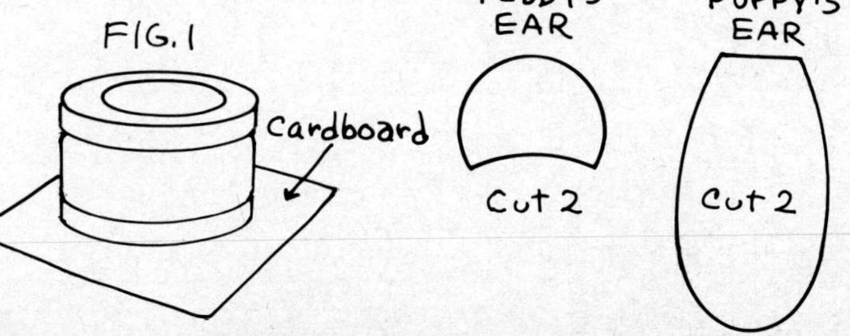

Angel Trio

Pictured on Page 4

Materials

4 wood napkin rings, 1¾″ dia. x 1¼″ wide
3 lg. (36.5 mm) wooden head beads
6, 3″ wooden spoons
Lightweight cardboard
Wood glue or white craft glue
Acrylic paints: orchid, yellow, white, pink, rose
Felt markers: black, red

Instructions

1. For the body, glue a napkin ring to a small piece of lightweight cardboard as shown in Fig. 1. When the glue is dry, trim the cardboard to fit. Make 3 bodies.
2. For the taller angel, glue another napkin ring on top of the one glued to the cardboard (Fig. 2).
3. For each angel, cut 2 wings and 2 hands from wooden spoons as shown in Fig. 3. An adult can cut the spoons with sturdy scissors for the younger children.
4. Glue the wings to the back of the body as shown in Fig. 4. Glue the hands to the front of the body, gluing the base of the hands only so they are not completely flat. The tips of their hands should touch each other. If you want these to be just angel figures, glue the heads beads in place. If you wish to use the little angels as containers, do not glue the head beads in place, simply sit them in place.
5. Paint the face and hands pink, the body orchid, the hair yellow, and the wings white. Use the pattern to help draw the faces on the head beads with felt markers. To trim the dress, dip the handle of the paint brush into rose paint and touch it to the dress to make a dot— make clusters of 3 dots for flowers here and there around the dress. Do the same to make flowers in their hair, making 2 rose flowers and one orchid flower. Add a white dot for flower center in the middle of each flower.

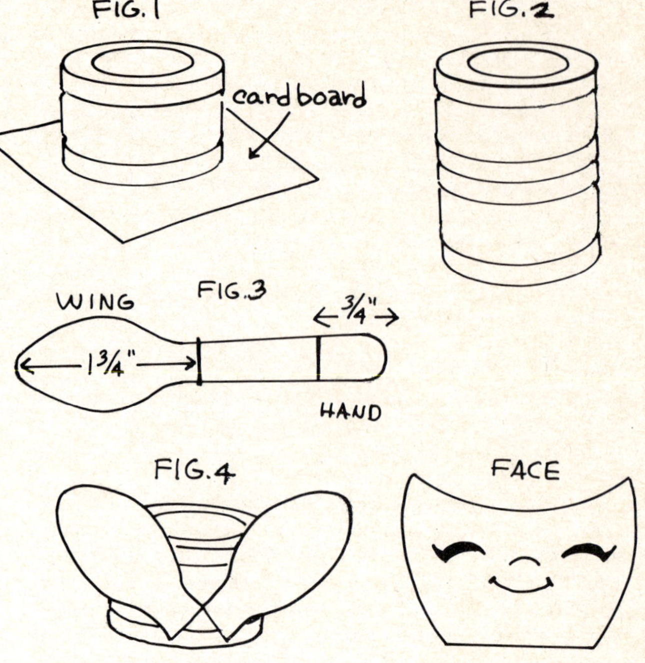

Noah's Ark

Pictured on Page 9

Materials

For Ark
29 craft sticks
Acrylic paint: red, green, yellow
White glue
Picture hanger

For Animals
4 or 5 index cards*
Sm. pcs. felt: brown, tan, gray, yellow, white, orange*
3, 10 mm oval eyes
Black paper
Craft glue
Felt markers: black, brown
Sm. (3/16″) paper punch

*Animals can also be made from lightweight cardboard and painted or colored with crayons.

Instructions For Ark

1. For the house section, glue 9 craft sticks together edge to edge as shown in Fig. 1.
2. For the center section of the boat, glue 6 sticks together as shown in Fig. 2. Cut one craft stick to 1½″ long and glue it to the lower end as shown in the diagram. To cut the stick, use a craft knife to score the stick, then break it on the scored line. This step should be done by an adult.
3. For each side front of boat, glue 6 sticks together using the pattern as a positioning guide. Make 2 and turn one over.
4. Assemble the parts as shown in Fig. 3. Glue the side fronts of the boat on top of the center section of boat. Glue the house behind the center section. For a roof, glue one stick across the top of the house section.
5. Paint the roof red, the house yellow, and the boat section green. Attach a hanger to the back.

Instructions For Animals

1. Using the patterns, draw the animals on index cards. Glue felt to the index cards and cut out each part. (See the patterns to know what color of felt to glue to the animals.)
2. To add dimension, draw the giraffe's head, the zebra's head, tiger's head, hippo's head, elephant's ear, lion's head and mane, and the monkey's face and leg on additional index cards. Glue felt to these parts, then cut out each one. Glue these parts on the appropriate animals. (NOTE: This step can be skipped for younger children.)
3. For the hippo and the elephant, glue the oval eyes in place. For the giraffe, zebra, lion, and tiger, use a small (3/16″) paper punch and black paper to make the eyes. Draw all other details with markers.
4. The animals can be glued to the ark to make a plaque or they can be attached with velcro so they can be taken off for play.

Noah's Ark

FIG. 1 - HOUSE
FIG. 2 - CENTER
1½"
FIG. 3
HOUSE
Center
MONKEY
tan Face
Brown
TIGER
Orange
GIRAFFE
yellow
Brown Spots
ELEPHANT
Gray
HIPPO
Gray
yellow
LION
yellow Face
Brown
ZEBRA
white
ARK-SIDE FRONT   Make 2

The Good Shepherd & His Sheep

Materials

4 plastic-coated paper plates
Craft glue
Pompons:
  18, ⅜" white
  28, ¼" white
  5, ¼" yellow
Acrylic paints: blue, white, brown, pink
Felt markers or crayons: black, red

Instructions

1. Glue the backs of 2 plates together as shown in Fig. 1. Using the pattern, draw the shepherd on one of the plates, positioning it as shown in Fig. 2. Cut out the shepherd.
2. Glue 2 more plates together the same way. Draw the sheep on it, positioning the sheep pattern as shown in Fig. 3. Make 2 sheep. Using the pattern, cut the crook from the flat part of the plate.
3. Paint the shepherd's headdress and the sheep white. Paint shepherd's face and hands pink, and paint the shepherd's robe and the trim on the headdress blue. Paint the crook brown. Draw the facial features for shepherd and sheep with a felt marker or black crayon, using the patterns as a guide.
4. Glue five ⅜" pompons to the upper part of each sheep's head. Glue 3 of the ¼" white pompons on top of the larger ones. Glue four ⅜" white pompons evenly spaced down the center of the shepherd's robe and two to the end of each sleeve. Glue the remaining ¼" pompons to the shepherd's robe as desired. The pompons can be omitted and the shepherd trimmed with rickrack, beads, or paint instead.

Noah's Ark

The Good Shepherd & His Sheep

Friend of the Desert

Friend of the Desert

Pictured on page 9

Materials

45 Skill Sticks*
Lightweight cardboard
Wood glue or white craft glue
Acrylic paints: blue, yellow, buttercup (goldish yellow),
  red
Black marker or crayon

*Skill Sticks are craft sticks that are pre-scored for easy
  breaking and have notches for building. When building,
  apply a little glue in the notches.

Instructions

1. Following Fig. 1, break the sticks into the required
   sizes. You will need 15 whole A-sticks (whole sticks),
   8 B-sticks, 8 C-sticks, 3 D-sticks, 22 E-sticks, 17 F-
   sticks, 10 G-sticks, and 2 H-sticks.
2. For the body, glue 2 F-sticks in the outer notches of 2
   A-sticks to form a square. Continue adding A-sticks
   and F-sticks until you have 6 A-sticks and 5 F-sticks
   — see Fig. 2. Glue the other sticks shown in Fig. 2 to
   the top sticks, applying glue to the edges of the
   sticks.
3. To make the bottom, turn the body upside-down and
   lay 3 A-sticks across the opening, gluing them in
   place — see Fig. 3.
4. For each leg, glue 2 B-sticks to the body as shown in
   Fig. 4. Glue 2 E-sticks behind each leg to form the
   feet. Be sure the feet all point in the same direction.
5. For the neck, glue sticks together as shown in Fig. 5,
   applying glue to the edges of the sticks.
6. Cut an F-stick in half lengthwise as shown in Fig. 6. To
   cut the stick, use a craft knife to score it. then break it
   on the scored line. This step should be done by an
   adult for younger children.
7. Turn the first neck section over (it is shown in black in
   Fig. 7). Glue a half-F-stick even with the end of the
   neck. as shown. Glue the other sticks in place
8. Cut 2 heads from lightweight cardboard using the
   pattern. Glue the heads over the upper end of the
   neck. also gluing the upper part of the heads to each
   other. Glue the end of the neck section to the front of
   the body. Prop it in place or use tape to hold it until it is
   dry.
9. To make the bridle. glue E-sticks and G-sticks to each
   side of the head as shown in Fig. 8.
10. To form the blanket. glue E-sticks and C-sticks to the
    humps of the camel as shown in Fig. 9.
11. Paint the camel buttercup. Paint the blanket blue with
    red and yellow trim (yellow on bottom. red on sides).
    Draw the facial features with a felt marker. following
    the head pattern.

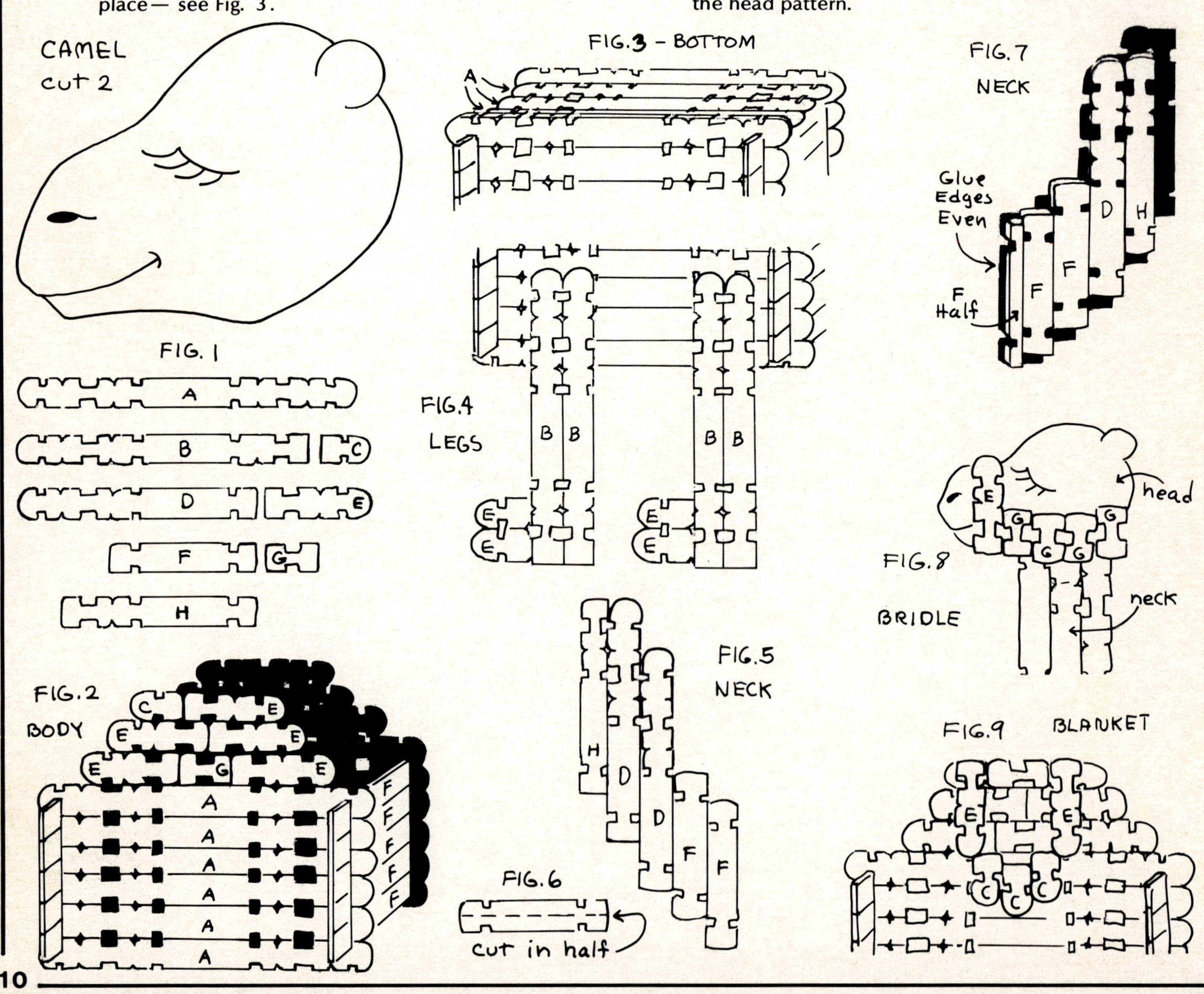

Easter Flower

Paper Plate Lily
Pictured on page 12

Materials

1 or 2 plastic-coated paper plates — white, if possible
2 craft sticks
2 toothpicks
1" yellow pompon
2. 6 mm yellow beads (optional)
Craft glue
Green acrylic paint; also white if white plates are not used

Instructions

1. Use the pattern to draw the lily on the front of a plate (see Fig. 1 for positioning pattern on plate). Cut out the lily and fold on all the broken lines.
2. Glue the tab to the first petal as shown in Fig. 2, forming a cone. Cut the small circle for the lily back, using the pattern, from a piece of the paper plate and glue it to the small end of the lily. If the plate pieces are not white, paint the lily white.
3. Cut 2 leaves from a plate, positioning pattern as shown in Fig. 1.
4. For the stem glue 2 craft sticks together overlapping ends as shown in Fig. 3. Glue the leaves to the stem and paint leaves and stem green.
5. Glue the back circle of the lily to the top of the stem, placing the tab of the lily at center bottom of lily. Glue the yellow pompon inside the lily.
6. Dip one end of each of the two toothpicks in glue and slip a bead on each toothpick. Cut off the excess toothpick beyond bead on end that is through bead. Dip the other end of each toothpick in glue and insert into the pompon (Fig. 4). This step is optional. The lily would look just as nice without this pistil.

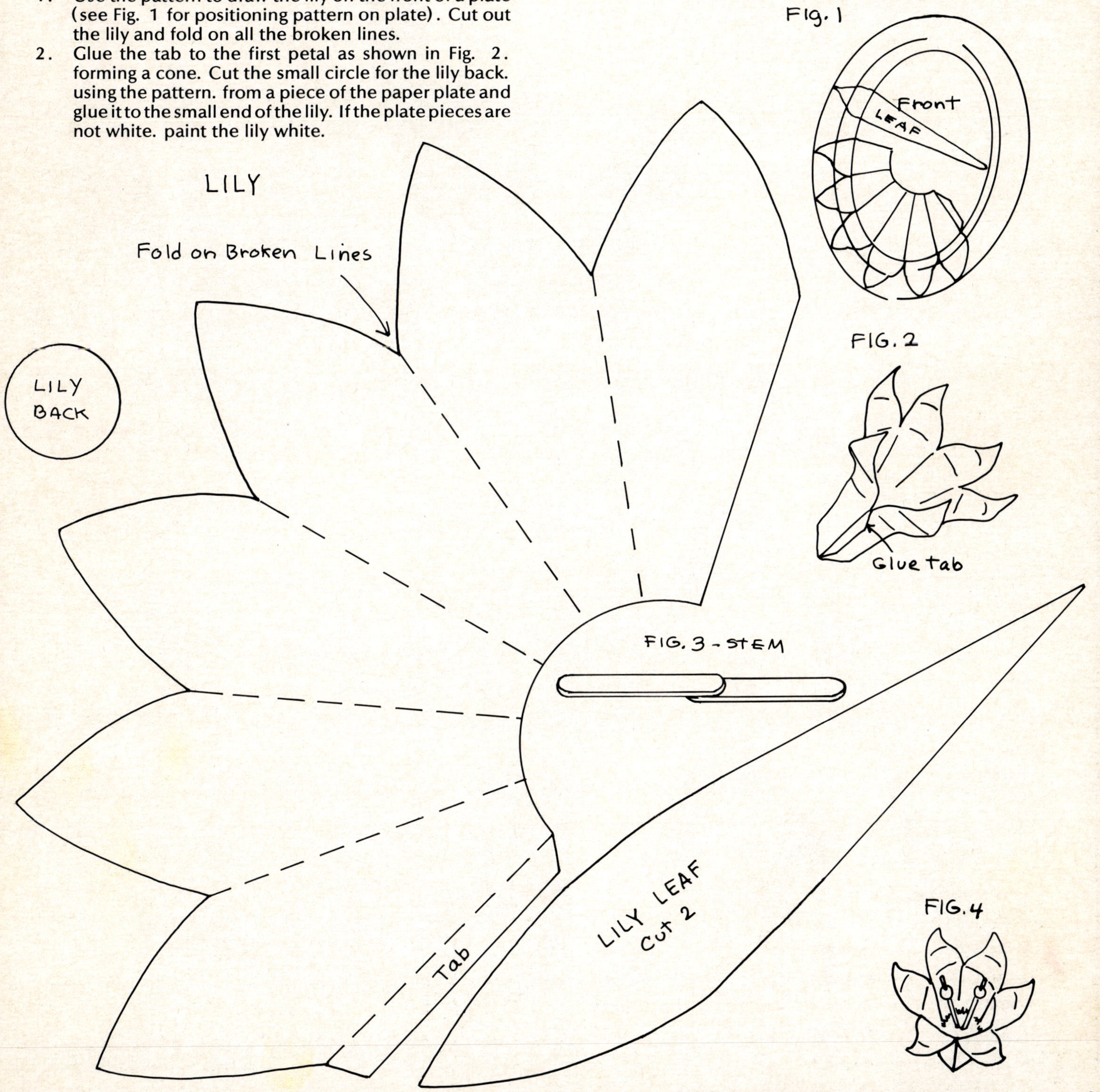

Easter Flower
The Pretty Church
12

Jesus Loves Me Plaque

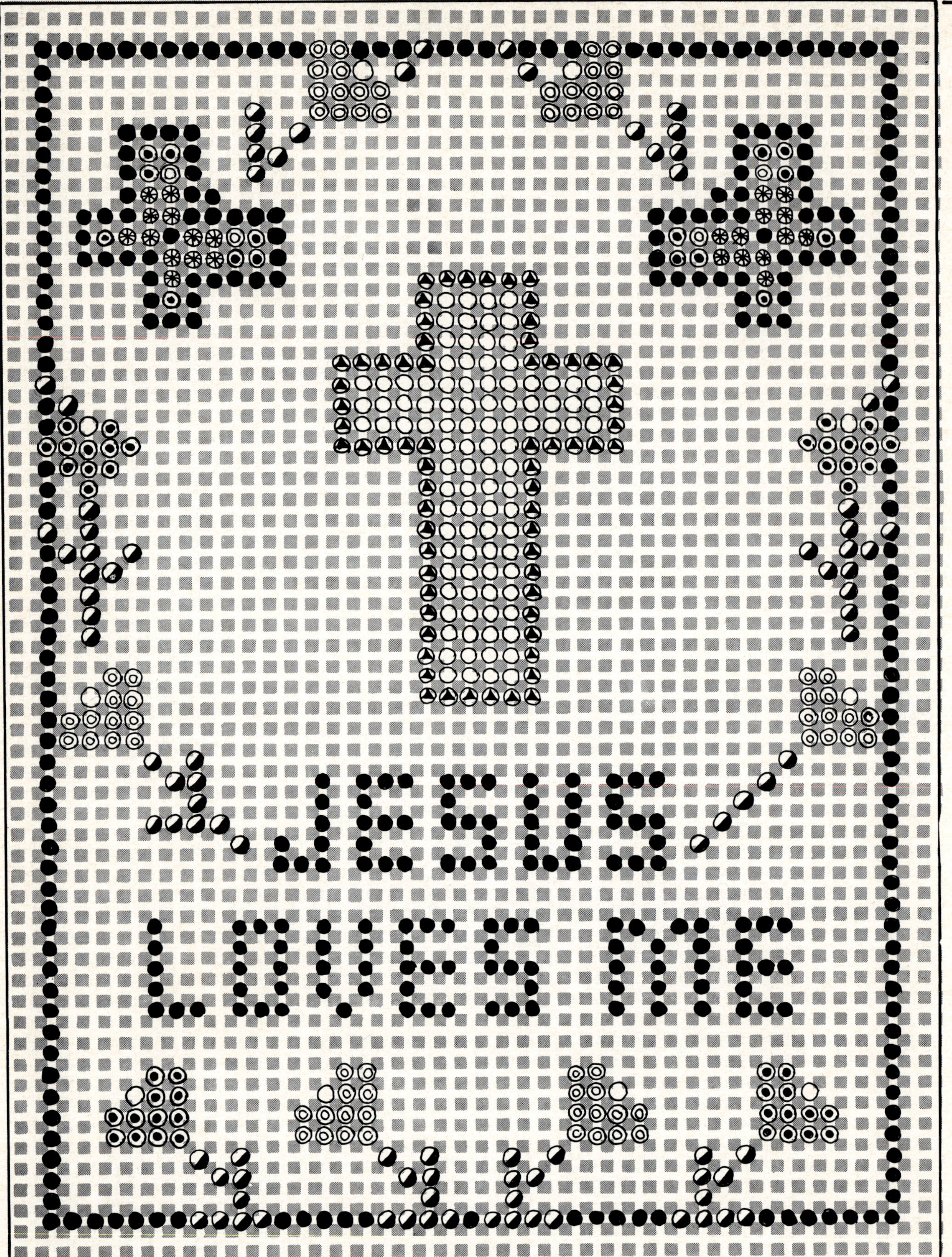

Jesus Loves Me Plaque

Materials

7" x 10" pc. 7 - mesh plastic canvas (found at most craft or needlework shops)
64 gold sequins
Construction paper: pink, blue, yellow, green, purple, orchid
White medium weight cardboard
Craft glue
Mod Podge Medium (found at craft shops)
Sm. (3/16") paper punch
Picture hanger

Pictured on page 13

The Pretty Church

Lesson or Letter Holder
Pictured on page 12
Materials
55 craft sticks
Wood glue or white craft glue
Acrylic paints: white, blue, green, yellow

Instructions

1. Following Fig. 1 for sizes of craft stick parts, cut 9 B-parts and 22 D-parts. Use the leftover ends of the B-parts for the C-parts; use the leftover ends of the D-parts or the E-parts. Also cut 11 more C-parts using both ends of some more sticks. (A-parts are whole sticks.)

   To cut the sticks, score them with a craft knife, then break them on the scored line. This should be done by an adult.
2. To keep your working area clean, work on wax paper. Assemble the front as shown in Fig. 2, gluing the sticks edge to edge. (Hint: To keep the door opening even, place 3 sticks in the opening but do not glue them in place.)
3. For the door, glue 4 sticks together edge to edge as shown in Fig. 3.
4. For the cross, glue 2 E-parts on top of a B-part. See Fig. 4.
5. Assemble the church as shown in Fig. 5. Glue the door behind the church opening. Glue the cross to the back of the church top. Glue the roof sections and window frames to the front as shown on the diagram. NOTE: If you wish to use the church as a plaque instead of a lesson/letter holder, attach a hanger to the back and paint it at this point.
6. For the lower front section of the holder, glue 6 D-parts together as shown in Fig. 6. Make a second lower section for the back.
7. Glue 2 D-parts on top of the front and back sections for braces, gluing the edge of a D-part between them to form a ledge for the bottom to rest on — see Fig. 7.
8. Make the bottom as shown in Fig. 8 by gluing 3 sticks edge to edge. Glue the bottom unit on top of the ledges of the front and back sections. Turn the holder upside-down and glue 2 more sticks in place as shown in Fig. 9. Only one stick will fit between the ledges, so glue the other one on top of them covering the space left.
9. Make a shrub as shown in Fig. 10. Turn this shrub over and use it as a guide to make a second shrub.
10. Glue the church to the center of the holder on front and glue a shrub on front on each side of the church
11. Make a tree as shown in Fig. 11. Turn it over and use it as a guide to make a second tree. Glue the trees to the back of the holder's back section.
12. Paint the church white, the cross and window frames yellow, the roof and windows blue, and the holder, shrubs, and trees green. (NOTE: The windows are simply the areas between the frame pieces (E-parts).

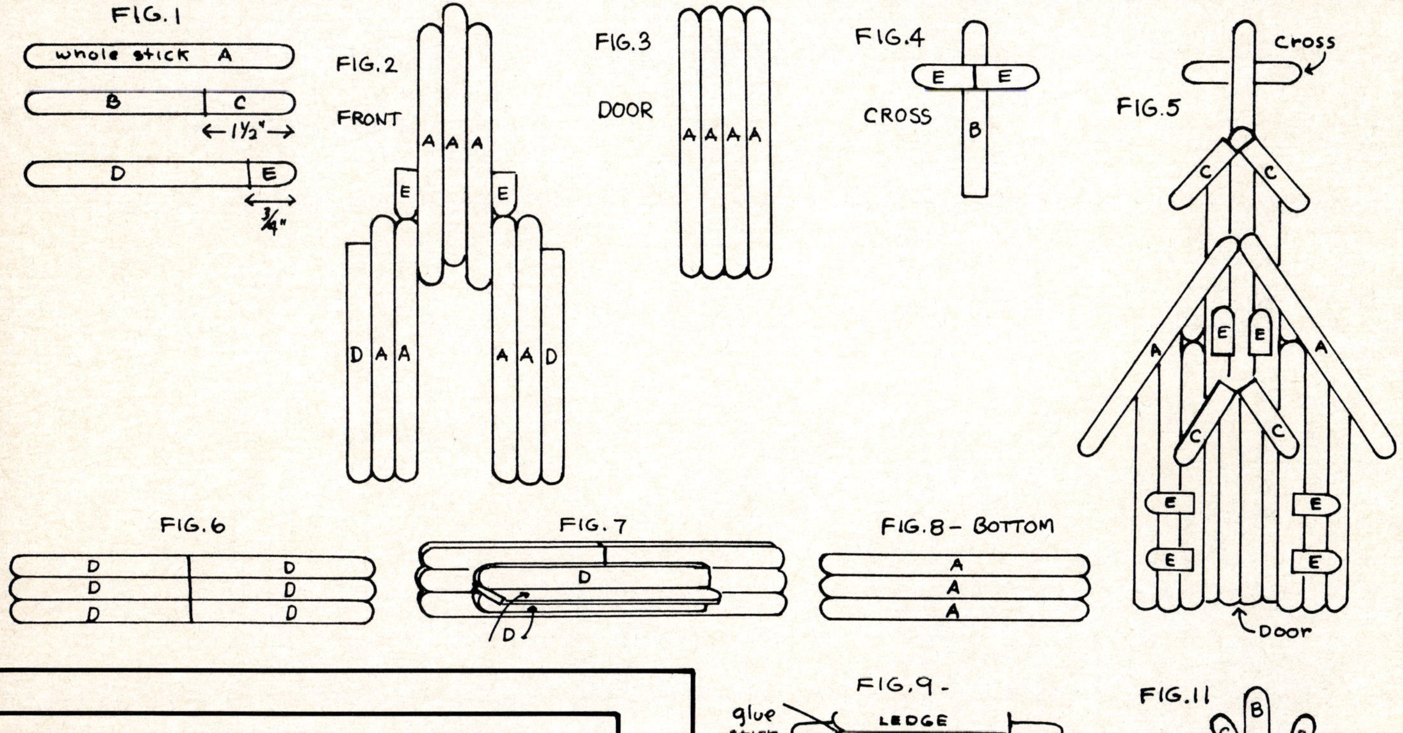

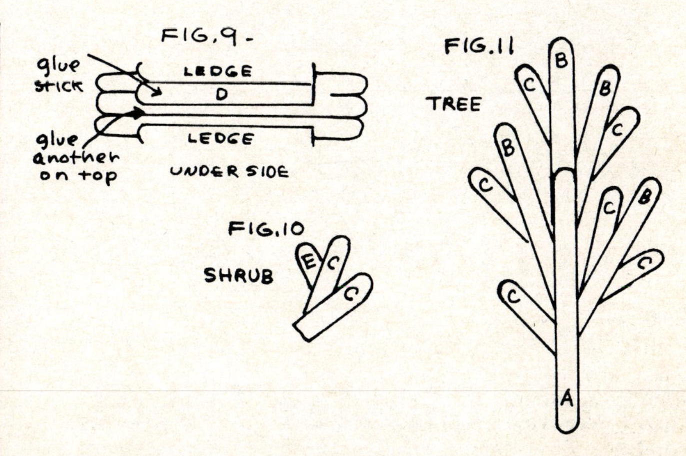

Create a Cross
Strung For Fun
Grape Cluster Trivet

Create a Cross

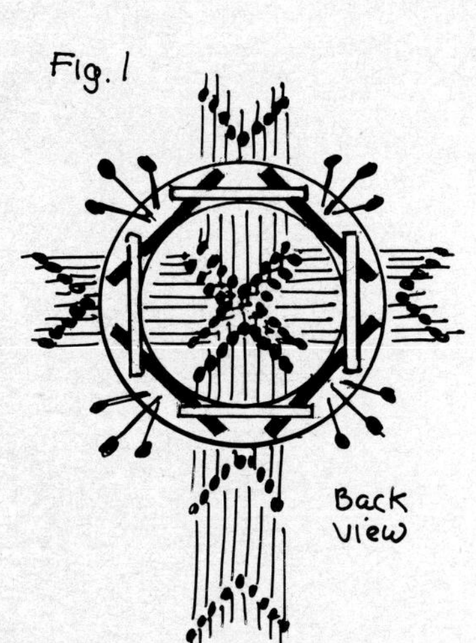

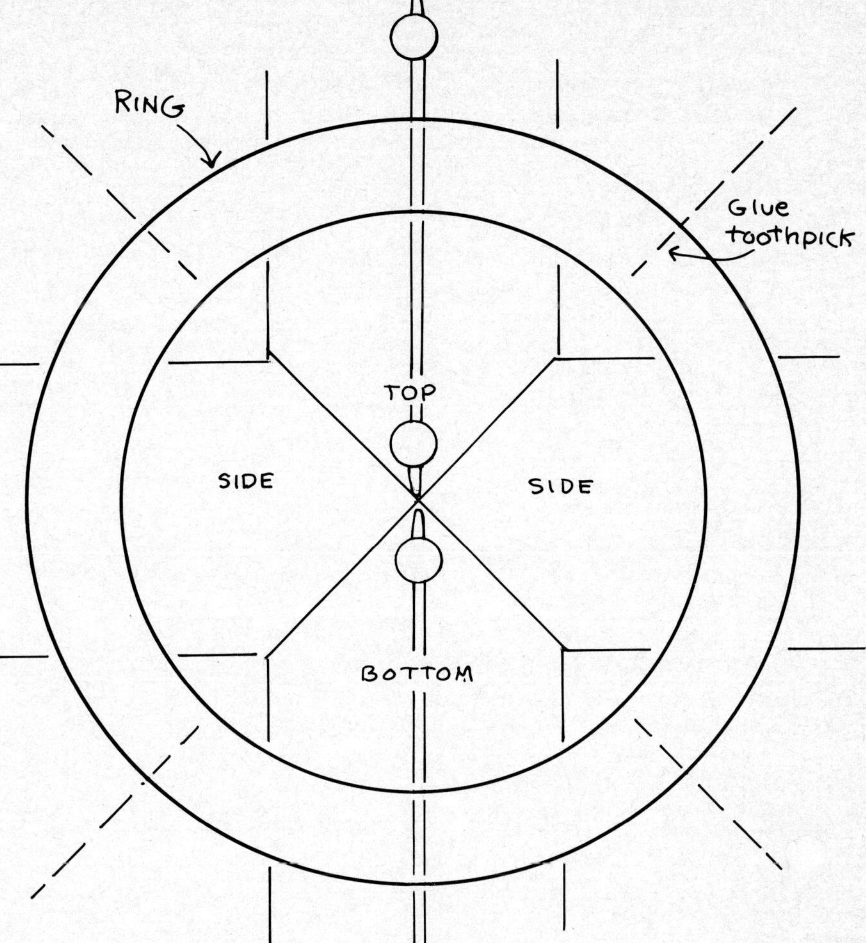

Materials

60 round toothpicks
8 mm beads: 81 rose, 12 pink
Acrylic paint, eggshell color
Craft glue
Lightweight cardboard

Instructions

1. Use the pattern to cut a ring from lightweight cardboard. Cut out the inside of the ring, too. Paint the front side of the cardboard ring using the acrylic paint. Allow to dry.
2. Glue a rose bead on each end of one toothpick for the top of the cross. Lay the painted ring over the ring on the pattern and glue the beaded toothpick in place on the ring as shown on the pattern as the center top toothpick. Glue beads on both ends of 8 more toothpicks. Glue 4 of these toothpicks on each side of the center one, keeping the tips of the toothpicks even with the diagonal center lines on the pattern.
3. Make 2 sides the same way as the top was made.
4. For the bottom, snip off about ¼″ from one end of 18 toothpicks. Glue the cut-off ends of 2 of these picks into one rose bead, inserting the toothpicks into the bead from different directions. This makes a double-length toothpick with a rose bead in the center. Glue this long toothpick in place in the center of the bottom section, following the pattern. Make 8 more double-length toothpicks in the same way and glue them in place on each side of the center one the same as for the top.
5. For the trim at the corners of the cross, cut 4 toothpick ends 1¼″ long and 8 ends 1″ long. Glue a pink bead on the pointed end of each. Turn the cross over so the back is facing you and place it on the pattern. Glue the 1¼″ toothpicks in place on the broken lines. Glue the shorter ones on each side of the longer ones.
6. For strengthening the back and making a hanger, cut 8 toothpicks 1¾″ long. Remove both pointed ends. Glue 4 of these to the back of the cross shown in black on Fig. 1. Glue the other 4 on top of the ends of the first ones as shown in Fig. 1. The top one can be rested on a nail for hanging.

Grape Cluster Trivet

Pictured on page 16

This is a good illustration when talking about the story of Jesus turning the grape juice into wine. It also makes a wonderful present for Mother.

Materials

Lightweight cardboard
Felt: purple, dk. green, lt. green
Green yarn
Craft glue

Instructions

1. Use the patterns to cut one large circle for the trivet, 19 grapes, and 5 leaves from lightweight cardboard.
2. Glue the trivet circle to an uncut piece light green felt, the grapes to purple felt, and the leaves to dark green felt. Allow glue to dry. Then trim around all the cardboard pieces, cutting the felt into the same shape as the cardboard glued to it. Turn the trivet over and glue light green felt to the other side, too. Trim the felt to fit the trivet.
3. Starting with the top row, glue the grapes in place. Glue all other grapes in place, overlapping them slightly. Glue the leaves in place.
4. Glue green yarn around the outside edge of the trivet and to the scroll- like design lines on the shown on the pattern (these are tendrils).

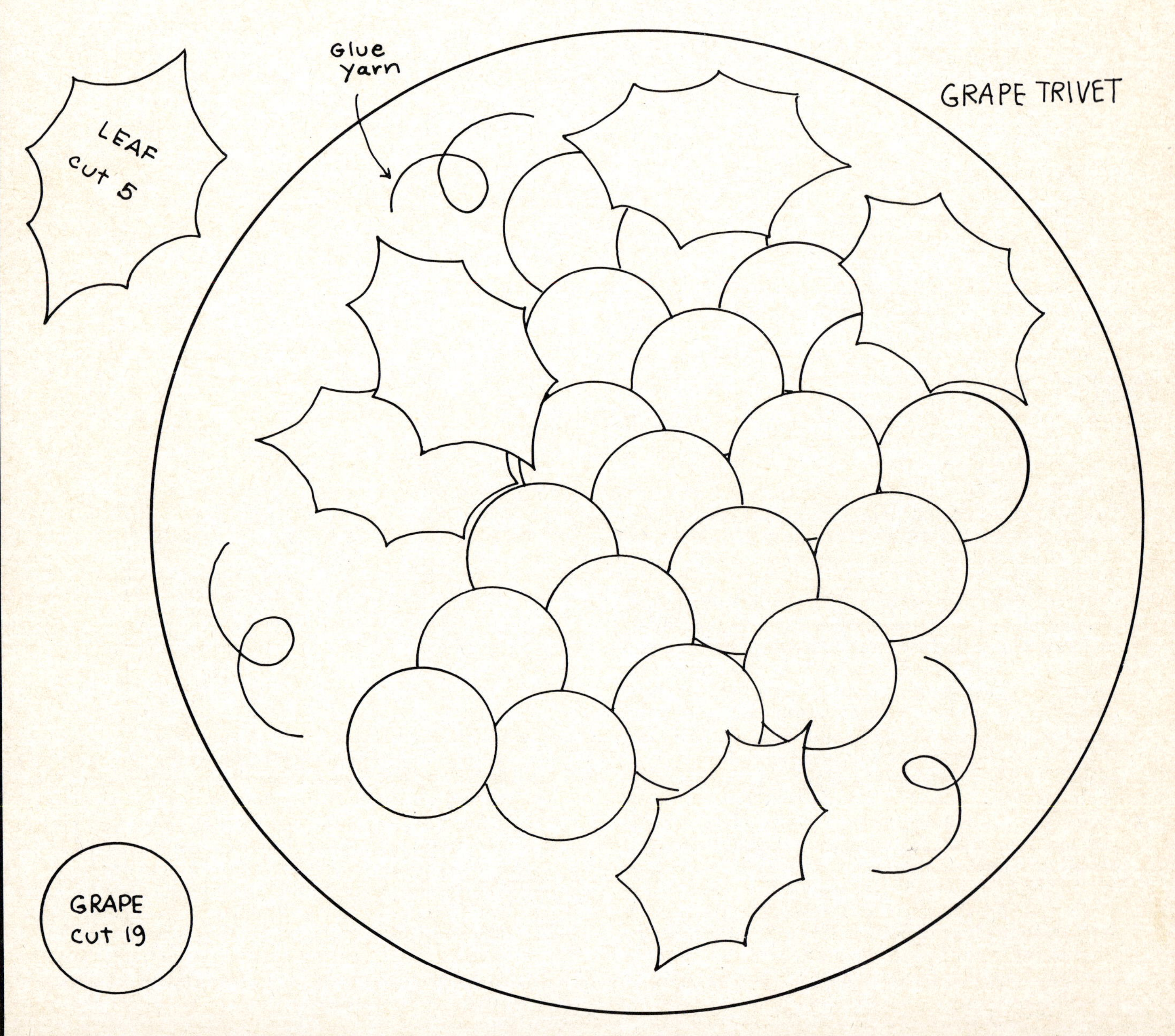

Strung For Fun

Beaded Window Ornaments
Pictured on page 16

Fish

Materials

1 yd. white covered 26-ga. wire
8 mm beads: 22 yellow, 24 green, 10 orange

Instructions

1. Bend the wire in half. To form a loop for hanging, twist the wire together about 2" from the fold. Separate the wire ends.
2. Begin stringing beads on one of the wire ends. The diagram key shows the color order of the beads to string. You will notice a solid line and a dotted line. Follow the solid line first and begin stringing the color of the beads shown. At this point you will just have a long, straight string of beads with no shape. When you have finished stringing all the colors of beads on the solid lines, then begin stringing the colors shown on the dotted line. Some of the beads on the dotted line will be some of the same beads strung on the solid line. Go thru these same beads with this wire end, usually from the opposite direction, and this will form the shape of the item.
3. Cut off the excess wire from each end. Shape the fish using the diagram as a guide.

Flower

Materials

1 yd. white covered 26-ga. wire
8 mm beads: 5 yellow, 6 pink, 25 rose, 32 green

Instructions

Make the flower by the same instructions given for the fish, following the flower diagram and color key.

Butterfly

Materials

1 yd. white covered 26-ga. wire
8 mm beads: 20 yellow, 29 turquoise, 40 orange

Instructions

1. Bend the wire in half to find the center of the wire.
2. Begin stringing beads on one of the wire ends. The diagram key shows the color order of the beads to string. You will notice a solid line and a dotted line. Follow the solid line first and begin stringing the color of the beads shown, moving the first bead up to the center of the wire where the bend is. Complete stringing all the beads shown on the solid line. At this point you will just have a long, straight string of beads with no shape. When you have finished stringing all the colors of beads on the solid lines, then begin stringing the colors shown on the dotted line. Some of the beads on the dotted line will be some of the same beads strung on the solid line. Go thru these same beads with this wire end, usually from the opposite direction, and this will form the shape of the item.
3. Cut off the excess wire from each end. Shape the butterfly using the diagram as a guide.
4. To make a looping for hanging the butterfly, make a 2" loop with a 7" piece of wire by twisting the ends together. Insert the ends into the butterfly as shown in Fig. 1. Cut off any excess wire at both ends.

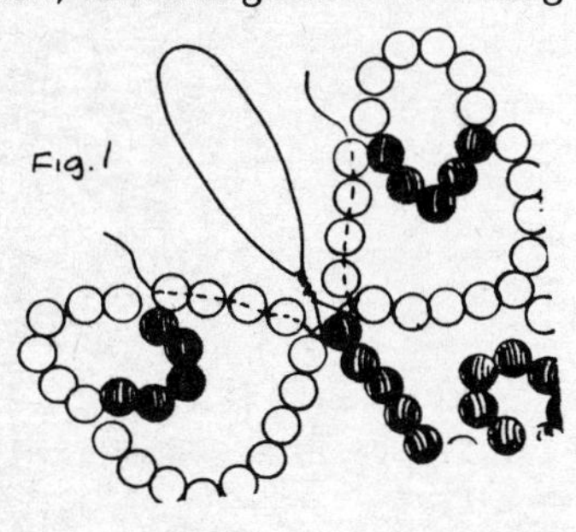

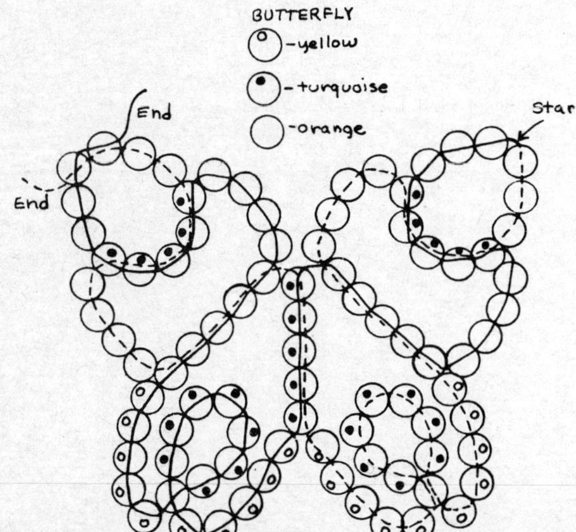

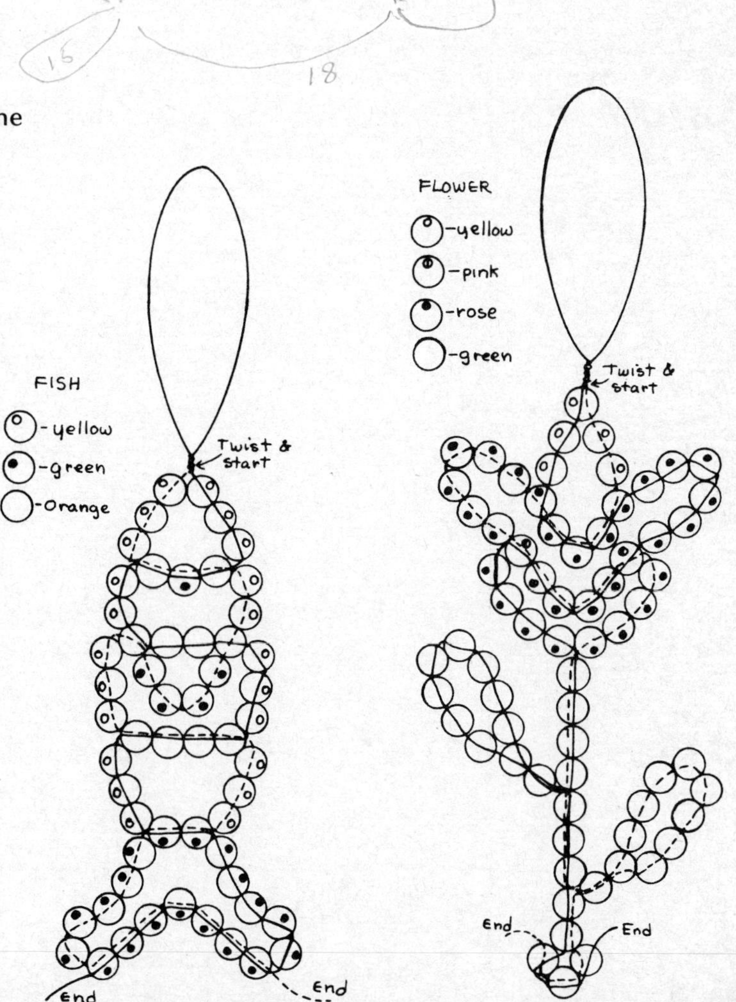

Jonah's Whale of a Bank

**You can keep coins or other small items in your Big Fish.
Or you can add a yarn loop to the mouth and hang him up,
letting him hold pencils and rulers for you.**

Materials

1½ squares of blue felt
Sm. pcs. black and pink felt
1 sheet 7-mesh plastic canvas
Crochet cotton and needle
Craft glue
White acrylic paint (optional)

Instructions

1. Following the pattern, cut one fish including the tail
   for the bottom from plastic canvas. For the sides cut
   two pieces without the tail.
2. Glue the sides and bottom to blue felt, applying glue
   to the outside row of mesh. When the glue is dry, trim
   the felt to fit the canvas. It is not necessary to trim it to
   fit each individual square of the canvas.
3. Turn the bottom piece over and glue another piece of
   blue felt to the tail and a piece of pink felt to the front
   end. When dry, cut off the excess felt.
4. For the center seam, thread crochet cotton onto
   needle and sew the top edge of the 2 sides together as
   shown in Fig. 1. Then spread the lower edges of the
   sides apart and sew one side to each edge of the
   bottom piece, leaving the front end unsewn between
   the X's. This forms the mouth. If desired, the edges of
   the mouth and tail can also be overcast with crochet
   cotton.
5. Optional: Cut ¾"-wide strips of blue felt and glue
   over each seam, stretching the felt strips for a smooth
   fit. Trim the strips to fit.
6. Using the pattern, cut 2 eyes from black felt and glue
   one to each side of the fish. If desired, add white dots
   of paint to the eyes for highlights.

Jonah's Whale of a Bank

Bible Bookmarks

Pictured on Page 21

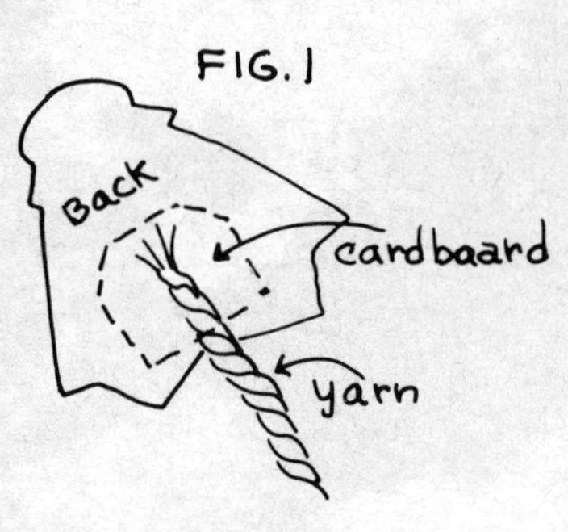

Materials

Lightweight cardboard
Yarn
Paint
Craft glue
Markers or crayons

Instructions For Shepherd

1. Using the patterns, cut one shepherd and one lamb from lightweight cardboard. Paint each as shown on the pattern. Draw the features and details with felt markers or crayons.
2. Cut a piece of yarn 2" longer than the book you plan to use the bookmark in. Glue one end of the yarn to the back of the shepherd and the other end to the back of the lamb. Cut small pieces of cardboard and glue them over the yarn (see Fig. 1).

Instructions for Boat

Use the patterns to cut one boat and one fish and make the bookmark the same as the shepherd and lamb.

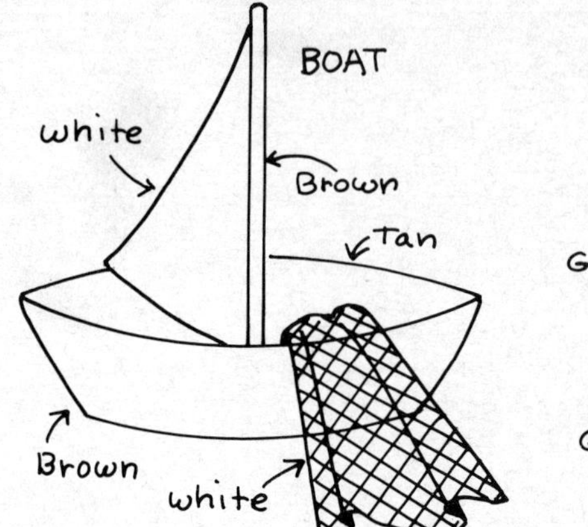

Joseph & His Coat of Many Colors

Pictured on page 24

Materials

Round can, 2½" dia. x approx. 4" high (cardboard type is best)
Approx. 23 chenille stems in assorted colors
Lightweight cardboard
Acrylic paint: pink, white, blue
Craft glue
Felt markers or crayons: red, black

Instructions

1. Cut all the chenille stems in half. Apply glue to the side of the cardboard can and lay a piece of chenille along it vertically (see Fig. 1). Place end of chenille stem even with bottom of can. Bend top end of the chenille stem to the inside of can and glue them in place. Continue adding different colors of chenille stems until the entire box is covered.
2. Use the patterns to cut the head and 2 hands from lightweight cardboard. Cut out and paint as shown on the patterns. Draw the facial features with felt markers or crayons.
3. Make the shepherd's crook by looping one end of a chenille stem half over your finger. Glue short pieces of chenille to the base of the hands for cuffs and across the smallest part of the headdress for a band. Bend the ends of the chenille to the back of the cardboard parts.
4. Glue the lower part of the head to the upper inside of the can. Glue the crook to the front of the body and glue the hands in place on the coat area with one hand over the crook; glue just the base of hands to the chenille so that the hands are not completely flat.

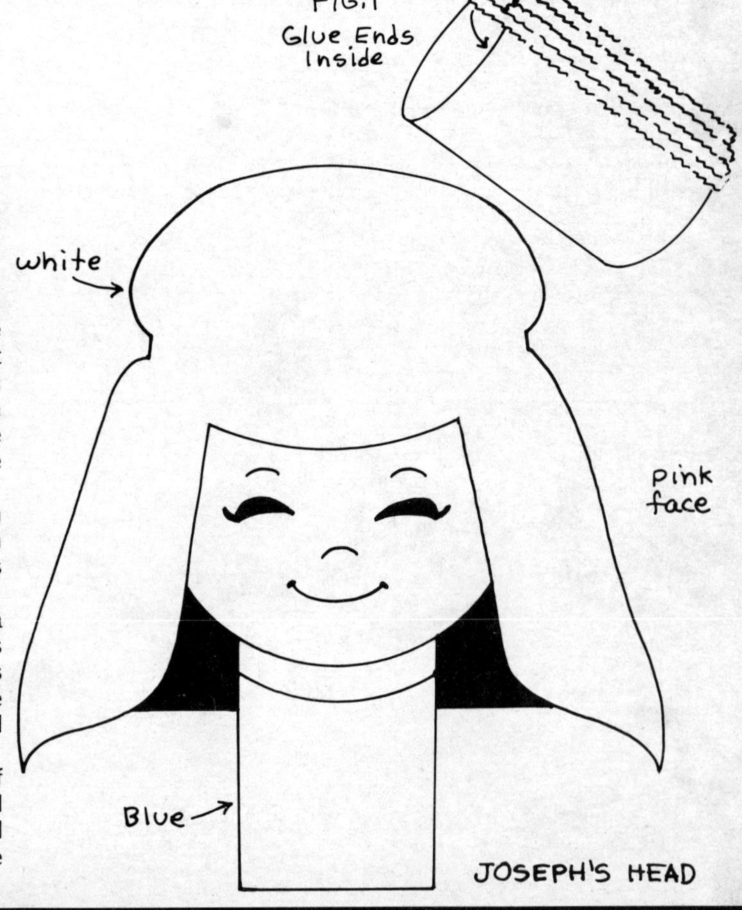